Never Meant to Be Alone

Never Meant to Be Alone

How Singleness Points to Union with Jesus

Justin Hendrix

FOREWORD BY
D. J. Marotta

WIPF & STOCK · Eugene, Oregon

NEVER MEANT TO BE ALONE
How Singleness Points to Union with Jesus

Wipf & Stock
An Imprint of Wipf and Stock Publishers
199 W. 8th Ave., Suite 3
Eugene, OR 97401

www.wipfandstock.com

PAPERBACK ISBN: 979-8-3852-2645-0
HARDCOVER ISBN: 979-8-3852-2646-7
EBOOK ISBN: 979-8-3852-2647-4

VERSION NUMBER 12/26/24

To Ed and Beth Hendrix
What a blessing it is to have good parents.

Contents

Foreword

Waiting is Never Wasted

THE CHURCH IS ALWAYS IN ADVENT.

Which is to say, the church is always awaiting the return of our Lord Jesus.

Christians are, therefore, a waiting people.

We are the bride; richly adorned, clothed in splendor, eagerly leaning forward in hopeful expectation to greet our beloved.

How shall we wait?

What does it look like to wait well?

Waiting for just about anything can not only feel painful, it can also feel pointless. Our society does not imagine that waiting could be of much use to anyone. Consider how the late Dr. Seuss describes the "waiting place" in his cheerful book, *Oh, The Places You'll Go!*

> . . . *a most useless place,*
> *The waiting place.*
> . . . *for people just waiting.*
> *Waiting for a train to go*
> *Or a bus to come, or a plane to go*

Or the mail to come, or the rain to go
Or the phone to ring, or the snow to snow
Or the waiting around for a Yes or No
Or waiting for their hair to grow.
Everyone is just waiting.
Waiting for the fish to bite
Or waiting for the wind to fly a kite
Or waiting around for Friday night
Or waiting, perhaps, for their Uncle Jake
Or a pot to boil, or a Better Break
Or a string of pearls, or a pair of pants
Or a wig with curls, or Another Chance.
Everyone is just waiting.
No! That's not for you!
Somehow you'll escape
All that waiting and staying
You'll find the bright places
Where the Boom Bands are playing . . .

The impatient child within us agrees. Waiting is the worst! I must escape this horrible, useless waiting and make something happen!

But is waiting only an in-between space to be escaped?

Does waiting *itself* have a use, a purpose?

Waiting is only useless if the thing for which you are waiting is of no use. Standing in line 9 minutes to purchase dental floss may not hold much deep meaning (apologies dentists). But standing in line 5 hours for a Taylor Swift Eras Tour Concert in L.A. may feel like the culmination of your existence!

It all depends on what you are waiting for.

The church awaits the return of the King, our groom, the Lord Jesus. So what is the purpose of our waiting? To prepare us to meet our betrothed. As each of us that comprise the body of the church goes about our waiting, we do so in two distinctly different, but equally valuable and important modes: single and married.

Both single and married Christians are waiting for their true spouse, but they practice their waiting in different ways. Single Christians practice their waiting by offering their bodies in chastity and their hearts in fidelity directly to Christ. Married Christians practice their waiting by offering their bodies in intimacy and their hearts in union to their spouse in anticipation of one day offering these directly to Christ.

Both are waiting, but in different modes.

This is both a challenge and a comfort to single and married folk alike as both are prone to think of married status as having "arrived."

The waiting-ness of the Christian life challenges single folk by asking them, "For what are you really waiting?" In a different way, the Advent nature of the Christian life challenges married folk by asking them, "Do you really think you've arrived? Even if you've given yourself to a good spouse, aren't you, at a deep level, still waiting?"

And yet, it's not all challenge. There is much comfort. The Christian faith dignifies the single life in more profound ways than any other religion or system of meaning-making—your waiting is not wasted. The married life is also celebrated in the Christian faith more than any other—as a foretaste of the future marriage supper of the Lamb.

For all of us who call on the name of Jesus, waiting is imbued with meaning and purpose.

With all due respect to the good Doctor, he is entirely wrong. The waiting place is not a useless place. The waiting place is where we prepare to meet the one we love, the one who most truly loves us. Therefore the waiting place is where the work happens. It's where we grow, change, become, mature, and flourish.

My friend Justin Hendrix has written a thoughtful, helpful, and wonderfully encouraging book that is for absolutely everyone. I hope it is read by students, young adults, single and married folk, parents and grandparents, pastors and laity. I was only halfway through reading the manuscript when I caught myself thinking, where was this book 20 years ago?

Well done Justin, thank you for the gift.

Single and married friends alike, stop waiting for the waiting to be over.

Start leaning forward, on tiptoes, to wait for love incarnate to come find you.

D. J. Marotta

Richmond, VA
Advent, 2024

Acknowledgments

There are many people to thank, but this is a short book, so I will keep it brief.

Thank you to my parents, Ed and Beth, for embodying God's love and modeling his character. Every step I have taken has always felt surer because of the foundation you built.

Special thanks to Rev. Dr. Gerald McDermott for his mentorship and guidance. Thank you to Rev. Jacob Davis and Rev. Ben Lansing for their helpful feedback.

Thank you to Church of the Incarnation. It has been a pleasure and an honor to serve you. You have given me more than I could ever give you.

Several times throughout this book I mention friendships that have been lifelines for me. I wish I could name you all here. Much of the joy I have tried to communicate belongs to you.

Finally, to Erin: it is an incredible joy to get to walk through life with you. This book and everything else is better because of you.

Introduction

SINGLENESS IS NOT EMPTY. That is not a novel statement; in fact, there are long and strong traditions in the church that have held singleness highly. Still, it often feels empty indeed. Even defining it makes it feel bare. It is difficult to describe without resorting to a negative: "singleness is not marriage." That makes it hard to articulate its value. Instead we defer to the freedom that single-ness affords. We show how it enables a person to be or explore or experience more. While there is truth to that, such an answer also evades the most basic questions—what is singleness, and what makes singleness meaningful? Like a tank top in the summer it is valuable, but only because it barely exists.

Marilynne Robinson writes that we "live on a little island of the articulable, which we tend to mistake for reality itself."[1] We tend to acknowledge what we can explain then deny the existence of everything else. I have struggled to see the value of singleness because I cannot express what it is. It is easier to say what it is not. This failure of articulation has consequences. If singleness is a void to escape, then the only appropriate response is to get married and get out of it. But that makes every subsequent day of singleness a day of failure. It offers no hope for the prospect of a lifetime alone.

1. Robinson, "Imagination and Community," 21.

If singleness is just an empty space to be filled, then there is no answer for the loneliness, anxiety, and disappointment that often burden it. Singleness can fit loads of hobbies, interests, work, service, etc. But can occupations and distractions give singleness worth on their own? Those are valuable, and singleness leaves room for more of them, but they do not validate singleness itself. Single people need to know that their lives have meaning—and not *despite* their singleness.

The single life might seem ephemeral, but marriage is obviously weighty. When you might be joined to another person in three months, three years, or even three decades, all plans seem tentative. Everything could change, because marriage's gravity is strong. As Paul warned his readers in 1 Cor 7, it immerses husband and wife in a flood of cares and concerns. Marriage will occupy all the space a life can give.

But what about singleness? How does singleness fill a life? How can the single life be more than a void to be filled with other things? How can a "nothing" have meaning or purpose? How can this emptiness be a place where God meets us, gives to us, and calls us to give ourselves away in return?

Those questions demand compelling answers. Fortunately, that same passage in 1 Cor 7 offers some clues. Paul does make much of the freedom that singleness offers, but the rest of the letter flips that freedom on its head. It is not a celebration of autonomy or self-determination. Rather, that freedom is an expression of the union with Christ and communion within the church that single and married persons share. Christians cannot equate singleness with solitude or isolation, because every Christian is joined to Jesus. If we are joined to Christ, then in his body we are also joined to each other (Eph 4:15–16). Together we share in the love of God. That means that the single Christian with no Valentine's date is not alone. Neither is the childless widow, the single parent, or the separated spouse. Every baptized believer has a bond with Christ and with fellow Christians that is deeper and more secure than marriage.

Besides, while marriage may be momentous, it serves to symbolize something else. Remember Paul's exclamation in Ephesians: "'Therefore a man shall leave his father and mother and hold fast to his wife, and the two shall become one flesh.' This mystery is profound, and I am saying that it refers to Christ and the church" (Eph 5:31–32). Marriage is a sign that points to that union with Jesus, not the other way around. However, marriage is not the only picture of that union. God uses singleness to show the beauty of this union, too. And, in a mysterious way, he gives singleness as an experience of that union in the present.

If that is true, then the struggle to name what makes singleness meaningful has nothing to do with its emptiness. The value of singleness is tied to union with God in Jesus. Its worth must be immense. It is hard to describe because its meaning is dense, not thin. G. K. Chesterton said that anything that can be considered in its entirety can also be imagined as small.[2] Anything we could claim to fully comprehend would be too meager to matter much. What if singleness is inexpressible because of its fullness, like a light that shines too brightly to be truly seen?

This inability to say what makes singleness meaningful does not diminish its actual worth. Its value does not depend on the meaning we assign it, or on how we use it. We are not responsible for creating that meaning, because the treasure within singleness is not something we can make. It comes from outside us. Singleness is a gift, and gifts have value that outweighs what we can see and touch. This is true for all gifts. It is even truer for singleness than for most other gifts, because the giver of this gift is God. He gives it to point to union with Jesus and to stir us toward deeper intimacy with him. That is an astounding claim, but this book is staked on that truth. It is the backbone for everything else we will say about singleness moving forward.

The first purpose of this book is to establish that vision for singleness. The second is to expand our desire for this God who can satisfy our longings. Singleness offers particular advantages for knowing him and seeing his goodness. It shows elements of

2. Chesterton, *Orthodoxy*, 63.

his character and purposes in unique ways. I have found this to be truest in the "waste places" of singleness. Loneliness, frustration, and uncertainty can foster a desperate dependence on God. That dependence can open doors and windows in the heart like little else can. Our goal is to see God's beauty more clearly from this place of need and trust.

Defining Singleness

Singleness can take varied forms. Some single people have chosen lifelong celibacy. Their examples are certainly relevant. They show that the single life can be rich and rewarding, even for those who are not on the same path by choice. Christianity has long valued this kind of celibacy, and the church has constructed a robust theology with which to defend it. In many ways, this book's thesis simply extends some of those claims to a different form of singleness.

This kind of singleness is not intended to be permanent—and often not desired at all. It is that precarious season of life inhabited by everyone who desires marriage but has not yet attained to it. That is what most of my single friends experience. I suspect the majority of single Christians would say the same.

It might seem normal to us, but this is a relatively new phenomenon. Of course, there have always been Christians who wished to marry but did not. However, dating culture has drastically altered the shape of singleness. Though it has given us unprecedented freedom, that freedom has mired many of us in a relational consumerism (and paralysis) that is difficult to navigate. Plus, we have all been saturated with stories about that singularly perfect soulmate, without whom we cannot be complete. Those narratives have complicated the process for everyone. This book, however, will largely leave those concerns to the side. This book is not about how we got here. It is about receiving from God with joy, wherever here happens to be.

With that in mind, this singleness must also be distinctively Christian. It comes with a call to abstain from all sexual intimacy outside of marriage. This goes against the grain of our culture's predominant postures toward singleness and sexuality. It also confronts one of the greatest challenges for single Christians. Sexual desire can present a formidable obstacle for anyone, single or married. When it couples with loneliness or insecurity, the battle only intensifies.

Although we may fail in different ways and to varying degrees, failure itself is universal here. So is God's offer of mercy and healing for those who repent. For many, the single life includes both wrestling with desires and struggling with past wounds. Those wounds may come from the sins of others, but they may come from our own sins too. A past relationship may have started well but ended badly. You may have crossed lines you fear cannot be uncrossed. You may have found pornography to be the simplest coping mechanism for your frustrated expectations. These are some of the places where the beauty of God's character will be clearest. There is no damage that Jesus will not finally heal, even if we have to keep carrying those wounds in the meantime. There is no loneliness that will not be met a thousand times over. God offers to satisfy the deepest of our longings, even when he withholds the thing we think we need.

With that said, faithful singleness is much more than the absence of sex. Jesus points us all toward more than a life committed to sexual repression. His example is a life of active love. It requires us to both cultivate and discipline our desires so we can offer ourselves in service to God and others. This kind of singleness affirms that those longings to give ourselves to a spouse or a family are good, even if they feel unmet! This is a part of Jesus' character that God wants his people to reflect, whether they are married or not.

That is an important point for understanding singleness. God does not call single people to stifle those longings. Instead, he calls them to a life of self-giving that incorporates others into a new family. This does not mean that single people are the church's built-in babysitters. However, the joy to be found in singleness may be hiding behind shared meals, on the bleachers at other people's kids' T-ball games, or in a local retirement home. As single Christians, we are not meant to give our bodies and our selves sexually, but we are still called to give ourselves away. It takes hard work to be single the way that God intends. Faithful singleness may be self-emptying, but it is hardly empty.

When I refer to singleness as a gift, I do so carefully. For much of the church's history, Christians have applied that language to those who vowed to remain celibate in service to Christ. That may have been Paul's intent in 1 Cor 7. When I call this more nebulous, unchosen single life a gift, I do not mean to equate these two kinds of singleness. However, I think that this unwanted or transitional singleness shows many of the same signs of God's generosity. God is certainly using it to achieve the same end. I have found that to be the case. I have learned more about the character of God, the gospel, and the Christian life from this singleness than from anything else. It has been fertile soil for cultivating contentment, patience, and hope. Receiving this singleness has meant learning to be loyal to the life God has given. It has required me to dig deeper into the single life in which he has planted me. That has posed a challenge, because often God extends his grace through means we would rather avoid. He has met me most powerfully in the singleness I want to abandon. God gives himself to single people in unique ways, even when we struggle to receive that gift.

I hope that this book can stir us to celebrate singleness. Marriage has ceremonies and symbols that make it visible. Weddings and anniversaries are milestones that everyone can recognize. Singleness does not have those kinds of markers. Maybe discretion dictates some of this. A feast may not be the most appropriate way to commemorate faithful celibacy. Still, I think this invisibility echoes our broader struggle to articulate what singleness is. I hope that we can recognize together that our inability to identify the truth does not affect its reality. As John Ames says in *Gilead*, "It all means more than I can tell you. So you must not judge what I know by what I find words for."[3] Nothing God gives is as meager as my best explanation would make it out to be.

---

3. Robinson, *Gilead*, 114.

Spoiler Alert

I wrote most of this book from 2017–18, while I was a single seminarian. Frustration supplied much of the original motivation. I was wrestling with a gift that I did not want (singleness) and with the desire for a gift I had not received (marriage). At the same time, I found that God was meeting me in those unmet expectations. He was using them to draw me closer to him and teaching me to rely on his goodness. I was learning to see his beauty more clearly from a single life I had not chosen.

In February of 2020 I married my wife Erin (just days before COVID shut the world down). Marriage has only confirmed the convictions that undergird this book. It is indeed a gift, and it complements singleness beautifully. Both gifts carry the same content—God's invitation to union with Jesus and communion with his saints.

I have done much of the organizing and editing work as a married man. Still, I have preserved the book's original character. It was written by a single person trying to receive a gift he never desired. I have not forgotten that struggle. Experiencing both gifts has made those original convictions firmer and clearer.

Whether you are single or married, may you see God's goodness more clearly in the gift he has given you. May the beauty of what he has given stir your longings for deeper intimacy with him. May you tangibly experience this union with Jesus as you wait for its fullness to come. His generosity eclipses your wildest dreams.

1

A Different Kind of Feast

"I HAVE A GIFT for you." That sounds like good news, especially if you trust the person who said it. A thoughtful gift is delightful. It fits, because the giver knows you. She recognizes your needs and your tastes. She values you enough to give something that complements you. The real joy is not in the gift but in being known and loved. On the other hand, everyone knows the awkwardness of an unwanted gift. A bad painting might come with an obligation to hang it in the hallway. An ugly sweater might mean an embarrassing Christmas next year. Not all gifts spark joy. Even worse, some people want gifts no one should give, like Mets tickets or leg lamps. Neither our giving nor our asking is always good.

I have found singleness to be a gift. That is the backbone of this book. It is also the source of the tension that made writing it seem so necessary. After all, this singleness often looks like anything but a gift. But if a gift from a close friend is sweet, and singleness is a gift from God, then how much sweeter should singleness be? We know that "every good gift and every perfect gift is from above" (Jas 1:17). We can flip that verse around, too. Every gift from above is good! Yet for many, singleness is an unwanted gift. It feels like a pair of cheap socks at Christmas, not like a well-chosen gift from a dear friend.

If singleness is a gift, then it must contain something that cannot be received any other way. To learn what that is, we need to see that singleness and marriage are not mere opposites. In God's kingdom they are tightly joined. We also need to see the purposes beneath God's gifts. So, to see singleness as a gift, we have to start at the beginning.

The Gift of Creation

Creation was God's first gift to us. He did not make the world as a hobby, or to be the terrarium for his most exotic pets. He certainly did not make humanity to populate his cosmic cocktail parties. There was no divine monotony that needed to be disrupted. Look more closely at who God is. He is Father, Son, and Holy Spirit. The three persons of the Trinity have lived in divine love for eternity. He does not need companionship. He does not need someone else to love, or anyone else to love him. Love is who he is and what he does, without beginning or end. Creation was not the solution to a problem. It was a gift that flows from that love.

That is a profound mystery. This holy God created a universe infinitely smaller than himself and exponentially greater than us. Yet the expanse between his being and ours does not isolate humanity from his presence. Instead, he has planted us in a world that pulsates with his being. He is near to us—to paraphrase Augustine, even nearer to us than we are to ourselves.[1] This world is wondrous because God's presence makes it bigger on the inside.[2]

He even uses this physical world to draw us closer to him. He never shuttled Adam and Eve to the heavenly places, or to some spiritual plane. Instead, God came down to walk with them in the Garden (Gen 3:8). God also used creation to sustain them. He did not intend for Adam and Eve to be self-sufficient. They needed food, water, air, and shelter—all of which God provided in the

---

1. Augustine, *Confessions*, §III.vi (11).
2. Special thanks to *Doctor Who* and the TARDIS for this turn of phrase.

world that he made. With his creation he nourished them physically and spiritually, in total dependence on him.

If creation is a gift, then its highest end is not the beauty or utility of nature itself. Its value comes from the one who made it, and who gives himself in it. Creation is worth more than the sum of its parts because its chief purpose is communion with God. God made the world so we could know him and enjoy him through it, and so creation could be known and enjoyed as his gift. Creation culminates at God's table, where God's people eat and drink in God's kingdom. Its highest end is the joy of being close to God. That is why the Bible begins and ends with feasts that God hosts. Everything between the feasts of creation and re-creation is a gift too. The creation feast is a celebration of this belonging and being with him.[3]

God gave the world to nurture humanity, but he also gave humanity to rule and care for his world. These two are tied together, because neither is sufficient without the other. Humans cannot sustain themselves without creation's resources. We would die. The earth cannot cultivate itself, either. Creation will not thrive unless it is tended by the sub-regents God has appointed to care for it. The plants of the field would not grow without human hands to care for them (Gen 2:5), and one or two pairs of hands would not be enough. Humanity needed to "be fruitful and multiply and fill the earth and subdue it" (Gen 1:28) to fulfill God's purpose. Because these gardeners reflect the image of the triune God of love, that multiplying and filling would have to flow out of love too. So, God packaged union and nurture together in the gift of marriage. Marriage was his means of building humanity to care for the world. Just as God's love brought life into being, this human love also flows into new life. That life, like God's, should bring flourishing to all that God has made.

This broke down when Adam and Eve wanted more than God gave. He had offered the whole garden as a gift. He only withheld the fruit of the tree of the knowledge of good and evil. But the serpent whispered that God was not really a giver. He claimed that

---

3. Schmemann, *For the Life of the World*, 17.

God was hiding something. He could give them access to knowledge that God was keeping for himself. Though God had only been generous with them, Adam and Eve followed the serpent's lead. They scorned God's abundance and reached for the one thing that he had not offered (Gen 3:1–7). But their new knowledge left them naked and humiliated. Now they carried a shame that compelled them to hide from the God who made them (Gen 3:8). By rejecting God's gifts, they had rejected God as their giver. Their relationships with him and each other had become corrupted as a result. That disintegration culminated in their exile from Eden and ultimately in death (Gen 3:22–23).

Two Impossible Gifts

Nothing has been the same since. Humanity's relationship with the world only dimly reflects its original calling. We do not fill the earth and subdue it in love. We do not tenderly cultivate it. We do not offer God's gifts back to him in worship. Instead we exploit his world for our comfort and power. Our relationship with God's creation has been poisoned to its core. So have our relationships with each other. Everyday tensions, violence, hurt, jealousy, and more make this clear. Sin has separated us all from each other, even in the most intimate places. The weaving of union and promise that would have made Adam and Eve's marriage—and their relationship to God's creation—so beautiful has unraveled. Now insecurities, greed, and mistrust plague humanity. Marriage has become a precarious and even impossible thing outside of Eden.

That is a grim reality. Broken humans cannot keep the promises that undergird marriage on their own. Those vows require a steadfastness that we do not have. This marriage tied to the world's flourishing can only survive if God gives it and upholds it. His covenants must be the grounds for ours, because our strength will not suffice. We can only promise to be faithful because God has reconciled us in Christ. We can only give ourselves to each other in life because Jesus has overcome death. We can only stand before God and each other without shame because Jesus' righteousness covers us. Grounded in that truth, marriage can be a bastion of hope, because it rests on God's faithfulness and points forward to a triumphant promise. Jesus is coming back for his bride. When he does, all this world's brokenness will be healed. Marriage is a spark of God-given light in a tumultuous world.

But what about singleness? How can a "nothing" be a gift, too? I am convinced that singleness and marriage are complementary gifts, not opposites. Both lead us toward the same reality. It is true that a husband and wife show the union of Jesus and his church in a unique way. Marriage offers a glimpse of the full union we will have when Jesus returns. It is a living picture of that reality now (Eph 5:23–32). It also relies on the promise that it symbolizes. Shamelessness, peace, intimacy, and harmony in marriage all depend on God. Only he can restore the brokenness that festers in our relationships with each other, and with him. Marriage's symbols, celebrations, and even failures lead us to this union with Jesus.

Singleness may be subtler, but it points in the same direction. It certainly depends on the same promise of union. At creation God said it was not good for Adam to be alone (Gen 2:18). Single people may not be completely alone—they may be surrounded by family, friends, colleagues, etc. Still, they walk in a certain kind of loneliness. Eve met a need for Adam that another Adam could not have filled. God's first answer to that dilemma was marriage, and single people have not received that. It is true that some willingly walk in that loneliness for the long haul, called into solitude for a given purpose. But most walk in it hoping for something else. They are waiting for that loneliness to be lifted and for that companion to be given. Many walk in it unsure if they will ever know another way.

It is truly not good for man or woman to be alone. God made all of his image bearers for intimate relationship, and in the flesh nothing approximates that the way marriage does. That is why the longings for marriage are so poignant. It is also why the single life often seems to lack something important. This is one of the most challenging parts of singleness. Some of the most frustrating feelings that come with it are not problems to be resolved.

They are not signs of defect or deficiency in the single life. Those feelings echo something true about God's design. God may not have given you that permanent companion, but he still does not intend for you to be alone.

Good news! Marriage is not God's only answer for human solitude. Nor is it his greatest one. Even marriage cannot resolve the insecurities and anxieties that often plague singleness. It does not eliminate those feelings; it merely transposes them into a different context. Loneliness can plague a married person just as easily, and sometimes more painfully. Marriage may lessen the likelihood of a Friday evening spent alone, but it cannot offer more than the love and promises of another flawed, limited human.

Only Jesus can fill what is lacking. You may experience singleness as a season filled with isolation. You may struggle with its uncertainties. You may feel like a water-worn rock as the rest of the world passes you by. But God has broken the powers of loneliness, because he has given Jesus. Those longings for intimacy, companionship, and love that singleness agitates can be fulfilled—but only in him.

It is simple enough to see how a single person's longings for marriage point to a need for union with Jesus. It is more difficult to see how singleness itself might symbolize that union. Fortunately, Jesus offered a window into the logic behind this mystery. In a disputation with the Sadducees, Jesus said that those who share in resurrection life "neither marry nor are given in marriage, but are like angels in heaven" (Matt 22:30). There are clear reflections of the single life in that verse. If marriage is a sign that points to the union of Christ and his church, then it has no place once Christ has returned. After Jesus comes, that union will be fully consummated. There will be no need for the picture (marriage) when the reality is present and visible. We can also see glimpses of the resurrection in the single life now. There is something about singleness that uniquely reflects the life we will share.

That might sound absurd, but here is the progression in that logic. In the resurrection, the need for marriage as a sign will be obsolete. It will be overshadowed by a kind of intimacy that marriage cannot rival, because that union with Jesus and communion with the saints will be complete. For Christians, the single life is beautiful because it rests in that reality now. Union with Jesus will be sufficient for all in the new heavens and new earth; it is sufficient for single Christians in the present, too. Singleness embodies that future reality. It testifies that there is no need for companionship that is not met first in Christ, and then in communion with all who are joined to him. A single person can wait and be content to receive what God gives, because the gift of Christ is enough. It is not good for us to be alone, but he has shared our bone and flesh to meet all of our longings for intimacy and communion. Singleness lives in total dependence on him, just as we will in the resurrection.

Refusing the Gift

God has infused singleness with a tremendous glory. Still, we have to confront the fact that everyday experiences do not match that exalted state. Though the single life may reflect the resurrection life, it is still one of faith and dependence. That foretaste of what is to come—complete satisfaction in the presence of God—is still a foretaste. Living by faith will mean clinging to that truth in the midst of loneliness and hurt. It will mean letting the invisible reality of union with Christ be the foundation that steadies us when the present is shaky and uncertain. Being joined to Jesus may solve the reality of separation, but those feelings of isolation or despair continue to linger. I still feel like life has bypassed me when my friends buy houses and have kids. I still have to fight bouts of jealousy at other people's celebrations. After all, there are no feasts or monuments to commemorate faithful celibacy. Singleness may be a gift, but its value is dwarfed too easily.

In circumstances like these, accepting what God gives and rejecting what he does not are challenging. All of us, regardless of the gift in question, are prone to follow Adam and Eve. God had given them the world and made them in his image. His way was a path that would have led them into deeper communion with him. But instead, in the serpent's words they saw a highway that promised parity with God. They took it, and it brought them to shame, disgrace, and exile. I am tempted to do the same. I could dismiss all that God has given in singleness and fixate on the one thing he has not offered. Rather than seeing singleness as a gift, I could reject it as the absence of the real gift and accuse God of withholding his best. Sometimes the present feels heavy enough to warrant that.

There are a number of ways to reject this gift of singleness, but I think they all share the same root. It begins with a refusal to be content with the life God has given. Some single people do this by pursuing marriage in unhealthy ways or by treating singleness as a state to be pitied. Others will resign themselves to singleness at the expense of good, God-given desires. Many will fill their single life with distractions that numb them to the pain of unmet expectations.

For many, the chief source of temptation will be sexual desire. When unmet desire rages, it is easy to see the gift of singleness as something intangible or distant. The companionship of a God I cannot touch can feel like a mirage. On the other hand, there are limitless opportunities to pursue intimacy or pleasure now. Singleness might seem abstract, but these temptations never do. Touch can warm the places where life feels cold. Loneliness could disappear, even for just a few moments. Living in a world that celebrates these solutions to singleness makes resistance even harder. Our culture largely believes that self-fulfillment is impossible without sexual fulfillment, and sexual fulfillment is impossible without sex.

But sex alone cannot offer anything like marriage's physical and spiritual melding of two people. It certainly cannot match the even deeper reality of union with Christ. Pornography brings a physical and emotional buzz without the vulnerability of real relationship. Sex can give affirmation, pleasure, and companionship, but those are short-lived if they are not rooted in God's promises. Physical intimacy without the joining of two into one that only God can forge is a bridge to nowhere. It gives fleeting stimulation but no hope beyond itself. Sex may look like the solution to loneliness in the single life, but it only recycles the disobedience of Adam and Eve in the garden. It separates the gift from the God who gave it, and it misses the communion with God to which real romance points. Refusing to settle for this parody of love is part of receiving singleness as a gift. None of the world's alternatives can match it.

Eucharistic Singleness

The opposite of this grasping is gratitude. The Greek word for "giving thanks" is *eucharisteo*, the word that gives us "Eucharist." In a sense all of the Christian life is eucharistic.[4] God has made us to gratefully receive all of his good gifts—Christ's resurrection, his Spirit, his word, the life of his church, creation, and more. That includes the single life. Like the food of the garden, it is a gift that God wants single people to receive daily, and with thanksgiving. Gratitude is the heart's way of recognizing that God's gifts are better than the things we would take for ourselves. It is God's cure for our souls' urge to seize what he has not given.

Again, that is easier said than done. There is no special technique for receiving singleness with gratitude, especially when the gift itself is unwanted. I, at least, have not found one. I only know the same simple ways we would receive any other gift from God. Participating in the worship and life of the church, obeying God's word, and submitting to the work of the Spirit. Learning the disciplines of prayer to unfurl the heart's sails and follow God's leading toward deeper intimacy with him. Receiving God's silence and responding with desperate persistence, like the Canaanite woman begging for her daughter's deliverance (Matt 15:21–28). Offering ourselves to people who have no claim over us, because God has already done the same for us. Learning to delight in the giver, even while we struggle to delight in the gift.

That might sound too simple to be helpful. It might also sound too difficult. You might find that it feels like a combination of both. We can learn to see singleness through the lens of union with Jesus, but I think most of us will still struggle to experience that union

---

4. Schmemann, *For the Life of the World*, 48–49.

in recognizable ways. Nearness to Jesus can seem elusive, especially when we think of that intimacy in an individual, internalized sense. That should not make us discount the reality that he is near to us. It simply means that we are still our parents' children. Like Adam and Eve in the garden, we shield ourselves from the one who made us. Though we are the ones hiding, we experience our seclusion as God's distance from us. Nearness to Jesus is something that we struggle to feel, even if we believe this union is real.

Fortunately, intimacy with Jesus is not something we only experience as individuals. We can know his nearness through our new brothers and sisters, too. This has been the biggest lifeline for me in singleness. Jesus has used his people to make himself near to me, especially when I have been the blindest to his presence. By digging into friendships in the church I have experienced him in tangible ways. Those friends have held me up when loneliness was heavy. They have known his nearness through me, too. After all, we were not made to be alone. Those individual means of opening ourselves to Jesus' presence are certainly valuable; there is a kind of companionship with him that we cannot know any other way. But drawing near to Jesus' people is just as important. If you want to receive singleness as a gift, rooting yourself in the life of the church and giving yourself to other believers is a great start.

Perhaps this is the most important point: nothing new is necessary. God has already given everything we need in Christ. All that remains is the opening of our hearts to receive what he has offered. The rest of this book will unpack what it means to do this in the harder places—where desire is unfulfilled, expectations are unmet, and the assurances of God's presence are all we have to hold onto.

2

Desire and Communion

THINK ABOUT SOMETHING THAT you want deeply. You probably did not choose to want it. You did not weigh cost against benefit when you first wanted it. Nor did you cultivate your wanting through a meticulous process of risk/reward analysis and opportunity cost calculation. But this wanting was not foisted on you against your will, either. The formation of our wants is much more complicated than that. Although we can choose things based on what we think and how we feel, none of those faculties is the primary source of our wants. There is a more nebulous undercurrent that gives them shape. It molds our minds, feelings, and wills, and it often seems impervious to any of our attempts to influence it in return. We can call this undercurrent "desire."

The church fathers talked about desire relentlessly—and often quite critically. They recognized that it can easily hijack a person. It has the power to drive anyone to great lengths, for better or for worse. Without discipline, desire can rage like a bull in a china shop. It can compel us to do the same.

In a basic sense, desire attaches needs to pleasures and folds them into the longings of our hearts. We need food, water, and shelter to live, but we also want food and drink that tastes good and to enjoy them in a comfortable home. Desire can also extend toward loftier ideals like beauty and justice. It can feed the ambitions that direct where we go and what we do. In its most notorious sense, desire is romance's kindling and fuel. That desire, when unmet, may be the most frustrating.

As unruly as desire can be, it also has a vital purpose. Desire ought to be a beacon that points to the God who made us and planted us in this world. Of course, we do not always experience desire as a current coaxing our hearts toward him. However, when desires function as they should, that is exactly what they do. God created us with needs that can only be satisfied in him, and he spiced those needs with longings that ache to be met. In Augustine's words, "You move us to delight in praising You; for You have made us for Yourself, and our hearts are restless until they rest in You."[1] God designed us to want what he gives so that we can learn to want him. As Schmemann writes, "Man is a hungry being. But he is hungry for God. Behind all the hunger of our life is God. All desire is finally a desire for him."[2] Desire, when disciplined and oriented toward the right goal, should draw us into deeper communion with him.

However, as a single person my desires often seem to conflict with God's gifts. Marriage is a gift, and God has given me a desire for it. I think I would like it. Yet that desire and this singleness seem incompatible. This desire for marriage often makes me want to reject singleness—or to accept it begrudgingly. Gratitude is difficult when my fists are clenched. This is not always a voluntary response, either. Anyone would rather be thankful than restless or frustrated. But when singleness is the hardest, or when the temptation toward envy is the strongest, desire can feel like a hindrance to the joyful gratitude I want to feel.

In those moments desire does not present itself as a gift that draws me toward the giver of all good things. It seems to stand between me and God instead. Frustration can cloud my ability to see what God is doing. Even worse, it might stifle my willingness to look for him. Still, I have found that this tension has yielded opportunities

1. Augustine, *Confessions*, §I.i (1).
2. Schmemann, *For the Life of the World*, 21.

for growth, and even delight. God has repeatedly met me where my desires and his gifts do not seem to match. In fact, this tension has been soil for contentment and satisfaction in him. I suspect that this is true for many single people. I also suspect that this reality is easy to miss. To see God's purposes in singleness, we must reframe this desire that often makes singleness so difficult.

Desire's Negative Side

Christianity has often been skeptical of desire, and for good reason. Desire may not be inherently bad, but clearly not all desire is good. More accurately, not all desire is directed toward appropriate ends. Theologians call this kind of desire "disordered." This can refer to desire that is oriented toward unworthy objects. More frequently, it describes desire for worthy objects in unworthy or inappropriate ways. For example, desire for food can be good. It ought to draw our hearts toward the God who sustains our bodies and delights our senses with his creation gifts. Desire for food as an end in itself (which often expresses itself as gluttony or snobbery) is disordered because the pleasures of food cannot satisfy the deepest needs of our hearts. Fixating on pleasure only entrenches the eater further in himself. This sort of desire does not move us toward our gift-giving, all-satisfying God. Instead it buries us in the trinkets, baubles, and comforts that dull our disappointments and medicate the aches and pains of life as sinners in a broken and intransigent world.

When desire is misdirected like this, it leads us to want things or people solely for the pleasures they promise. That sort of desire will quickly sour, because those pleasures will not satisfy. The unmet longings that follow will only foment more dissatisfaction, and we will inevitably respond in self-destructive ways. We will envy what others have, lust for what we should not want, and covet what we cannot reach. We will even respond to desire in ways that undermine the things we want most. For example, someone who substitutes pornography for real intimacy will instead stunt both his capacity for intimacy and his ability to wait

13

for it. Desire directed toward finite things—however good—will always leave us wanting.

Disordered desire is so intuitive for our sinful hearts that we struggle to conceive of desire in any other way. Still, Scripture does not condemn all desire. Psalm 10 distinguishes the desire of the wicked from that of the righteous. Psalm 145:19 says God satisfies the desires of those who fear him. Psalm 34:8 urges us to "taste and see that the Lord is good." Proverbs 13:12 and 13:19 praise the sweetness of fulfilled desire. Though Paul often speaks negatively of desire, he specifically contrasts the sinful desires of the flesh with the life of the Spirit (Gal 5:16–26; Eph 2:3; Eph 4:22). Those misdirected desires must be reoriented toward God and his gifts. This is a crucial part of the Spirit's work in our lives. He shapes us to love what is good, approve what is excellent, and desire God himself. That is God's antidote for the poison pill that the serpent gave Adam and Eve. Their sin was not just wanting something. It was wanting to become something God never intended them to be, and to be so independently of God. Their good desire for God and his gifts had morphed into covetousness. The desire the Spirit cultivates does the opposite. It shapes our hearts to pursue the only one who can satisfy our longings.

Desire, Singleness, and Longing Forward

With that said, it might seem like romantic desire has no place in singleness. After all, it appears to be a longing without a proper end, at least within the single life. Many might immediately equate such a desire with lust. It is a word rife with discontentment and dissatisfaction. It is hard to see how this desire could lead toward intimacy with God.

The roots of this desire are easy to trace. It grows from that problem God identified before Eve's creation— "It is not good that the man should be alone" (Gen 2:18). Many of us long for exclusive, romantic intimacy because God made us for this kind of connection. This capacity for relationships is part of what it means for us to be made in God's image. The drive for romantic relationships, in particular, reflects a need to live in union with and dependence on someone else. Adam could not fulfill his purpose before God without Eve. Nor could Eve without Adam. It was not good for either to be alone.

Romantic desire is an echo of that problem's persistence. Although God has established means besides romance to alleviate that problem, like friendship, romantic desire often resists that comfort. It can cultivate a kind of loneliness, or a sense of loss, that will flourish even in the midst of robust friendship. It can accent that absence with sharp stings. The loneliness that often plagues singleness can be agonizing because God did not design us to endure alienation or isolation. We yearn for companionship and intimacy because we were never meant to be alone.

That makes desire a two-edged sword in the single life. We look for the thrill of romance because God made us for deep relationships. That is good. But that unmet desire is likely the primary reason singleness can be so painful. How we handle it will largely define how we experience the single life.

We tend to deal with unmet desire through resignation or compromise. Most of us probably vacillate between the two. Resignation seeks comfort or peace by abandoning desire altogether. If the longing for marriage feels too strong or if it hurts too much, we can marginalize it or try to hide from it. We might pour ourselves into a career, or a hobby, or entertainment. Those may not be bad in themselves, but they are lousy means of dealing with desire run amok. Resignation might even try to detach itself from desire altogether. It is easier to dismiss marriage than to build the endurance one needs to wait for it. Resignation might appear to be a good option, especially if it frees us to pursue other good things. It can even look and feel like contentment—the elusive white whale of Christian virtues. However, resignation's greatest mistake is the assumption that desire is dispensable. It regards it as something that can be ejected when it is unpleasant, or jettisoned when it becomes a hindrance. It assumes, in other words, that this kind of desire is not a gift with a vital purpose.

Pornography and other kinds of sexual sin show how pervasive compromise is. Unmet desire is deeply painful, and we will often do almost anything to medicate ourselves to the suffering it brings. But the initial promise of fulfillment—whether from a screen, a touch, or even just a hope—gives off more smoke than fire. Compromise cannot satiate this desire. It can fuel it, but that only makes the struggle harder. It cannot bring relief, because it cannot reach what desire seeks. Our deepest longings are not for sex, regardless of what our bodies or rom-coms tell us. Sex may drive the strongest urges, but our true desires run much deeper than that. We want sex and romance the way a child longs to play in the gutter. Something in us knows that a great ocean exists, so we reach for the resemblance at hand and scream when it is denied us.[3] We have no idea of the true end of our longings. The same is true for sex. We want it because it is attainable, and because it boldly offers what we think our desires seek. Yet it can only offer a flimsy replica of our true need. Neither resignation nor compromise can give us the profound communion with another that our souls are wired to pursue. As Lewis said, "Indeed, if we consider the unblushing promises of reward and the staggering nature of the rewards promised in the Gospels, it would seem that our Lord finds our desires, not too strong, but too weak. . . We are far too easily pleased."[4]

There is a bitter irony to all of this. Desire, by nature, is endless. None of our compromises or distractions can satisfy it. They will only blunt our joy once we realize how far from satisfied we truly are. This is bad news for anyone who thinks romance will fulfill their desires. Regardless of how fervent that love is, or how long it lasts, there will always be something missing. Insecurity and selfishness will not let us fully give ourselves away. They will not let us fully receive anyone, either. Besides, all relationships will end with either death or alienation. They will not bear the weight of desire's unmet expectations. This is clearly true in our compromises. It is true in marriage, too. Marriage joins two finite,

3. Lewis, "Weight of Glory," 26.
4. Lewis, "Weight of Glory," 26.

flawed people. That fact alone belies the possibility of desire's fulfillment. The objects of our desire—even marriage itself—only
have enough power to point us to something greater. They cannot
satisfy the longings that they fuel. Desire might be a sign pointing
us away from ourselves, but signs can become snares if we never
follow where they lead.

Desire, Union, and Communion

Desire's purpose is not to fuel the pursuit of things that cannot
satisfy. It is to spur us toward the God who loves us, and who made
us to find joy and satisfaction in him. More specifically, it is to
drive us toward union with him. For Christians, union is not just
a theme or metaphor. It is certainly more than God's solution to
desire's problem. Union with God is the reason that desire exists. It
is its final object, its reason for being. Our desires should spur us to
be near him, to know him, and to be joined to him. They have no
use in the Christian life if they point anywhere else. Desire has no
place in the single life if it does not serve that end.

It is no coincidence that God has placed union at the end
of this desire. You could sum up our whole faith with that word.
A desire for physical union reflects important elements of the
character of God and his work of redemption. First, union itself
is an essential attribute of God's being. The Father, Son, and Holy
Spirit are eternally united in perfect love. There is only one God in
three persons, and he is characterized by union. We want union
because we were made to reflect a God who *is* union. Second,
union is at the core of our salvation. God the Son united a human
nature to his eternally divine person. Without diminishing the
divine union in any way, he brought that human nature into the
life of God. Theologians call this union of humanity and divinity
in Jesus the "hypostatic union." Here is a stab at saying this more
directly. Jesus is the Son of God. As the Son he has shared completely in the full life of the triune God for eternity. That means

that when Jesus was born there was, quite literally, a human fully participating in the life of God.[5]

Perhaps the greatest mystery here is union's place at the core of our relationships with God and each other. Jesus did not just take on a human nature so he could gain the ability to die. He did it so that our fallen, broken humanity could be joined to his perfect humanity. When he poured out the Holy Spirit he extended the offer of that union to us, so we could share in his resurrection life and be brought into the life and love of God. Through union with him, Christ makes his righteousness, inheritance, place before the Father, and resurrection life available to us. He even brings us into the same life and love of God. This is why Peter can say that we have "become partakers of the divine nature" (2 Pet 1:4). Jesus' humanity is infinitely better than the human nature we know and cling to, and he offers it to us.[6]

Singleness and New Humanity

That last point brings up something that is counterintuitive for most of us. The desires that shape the single life demand that *we* be transformed, not our circumstances. Consider how difficult desire can be in the single life. The problem is not desire itself but us. Desire is not incompatible with the callings God has given. *We* are incompatible with what God offers, and with the desires he has given to point us there.

I see this clearly in my own desires. Even when I desire the right things I fail to desire well. The Bible teems with images of desire fulfilled, and of a God who meets all our longings in himself. My desires, however, often seem to lead me away from God's story. My longings do not always match the gifts God gives in the present. Godly desire feels like an impossibility, particularly when the gap between desire and gift breeds disappointment. We need

5. Mascall, *Christ, the Christian, and the Church*, 92–3.
6. Mascall, *Christ, the Christian, and the Church*, 92–101.

our relationship with our desires to be reformed. We need Jesus' new humanity in place of ours.

Think of this new humanity that Jesus offers along vertical and horizontal lines. Perhaps the first is more obvious. We need to be transformed if we are to be right with God. I am guilty of sin against God; I need to be forgiven and cleansed. Shame and guilt cause me to flee from God's presence; I need the boldness of the Son before the Father. My sinful heart pursues the objects of its desire as ends in themselves; I need to see God as the only one who can satisfy those longings. All the barriers that stand between me and intimacy with God need to be broken down. I need Jesus to replace my broken human nature with his perfect human nature.

The second line flows out of this reconciling union with him. We need our relationships with each other to be transformed, too. Selfishness drives us to take, not give. Vulnerability and anxiety compel us to defend, not invite. Pride groans at receiving another's grace. Those pitfalls prevent us from knowing real communion with each other. If the single life in Christ shows a picture of a heavenly reality, then the single life apart from Christ makes visible what is true for all sinners. We are not meant to be alone, but we are.

Marriage may be a gift, but it is not the solution to that loneliness. It does not offer the new humanity we need. It is, however, a sign that this loneliness does not have the final word. That sign points us to union with Jesus, a reality we experience together in the life of the church. In baptism the Holy Spirit brings us into a new family. In the bread and wine Jesus forms us into a new body. This new people can experience communion with each other without boundaries or exclusion, because the waters of baptism are thicker than blood. In the Holy Spirit we have a bond that is stronger and tighter than marriage. It is a bond that we cannot break, because it is a union with and in a God who *is* love. You need what marriage symbolizes, not marriage itself.

This will be hard for us, for valid reasons. Others will fail to love us well, and we will return the favor. Even in the church we will sometimes experience loneliness. Still, Christ's presence in the lives of brothers and sisters can make the riches of God's goodness clearer. When the church reflects this union, those promises become believable. Realities that might otherwise seem abstract become tangible here.

The longings you might feel for intimacy and deep relationship are human longings. They are not, in themselves, responsible for your hurt or your vulnerability to sin. They are not obstacles to your joy. Nor are they evidence that singleness is a plague to avoid. You have them because your soul desires its maker like a deer pants for water. Do not deny them or try to marginalize them. Do not settle for this world's romantic baubles and trifles either. Instead, seek a new relationship with your desires. Recognize that even the most painful parts are signs directing you toward a delight in God that you could not otherwise imagine. Let that desire for his presence shape your life and longings. Let his Spirit bring the desires of your heart under his discipline.

Those desires shaping your singleness may indeed be painful. They may seem to undermine contentment and threaten peace. Nevertheless, follow them. Not toward the immediate pleasures they might lurch after. And not into the chaos they pursue when unfettered. Follow them toward the one who can actually satisfy the desires he has given. As you follow them, learn to recognize what God has given in the church. It is the true foretaste of the profound intimacy that we pursue in sex. This is God's answer on earth for our loneliness and isolation. It is a place of belonging that is given, not earned.

God has promised that union with Jesus is enough to satisfy all of our longings, and he has offered it as a gift. He is giving the single life as a picture of the resurrection life, when Jesus will fully satisfy those desires. But this communion that desire teaches us to seek is not relegated to some distant future. Its fullness may lie ahead of us, but it begins here. It is the very thing to which the single life points. That is true even with this heavy load of otherwise unmet desires. The presence of Christ that we long for in the future is also enough for us now.

3

On Disappointment and Contentment

Two thousand five was the one glorious year that D.J. Shockley started at quarterback for the Georgia Bulldogs. Many were skeptical that D.J. would succeed. I was confident, though—as a fan, and as an elite Xbox athlete. NCAA Football was a much easier game with a mobile quarterback like him. Besides, D.J. might have waited four years for his chance to lead Georgia's offense, but on my Xbox I would have as many chances as I needed.

Georgia's first opponent was #18 Boise State, with their potato-chucking quarterback Jared Zabransky. That was a tough opening game. I replayed it til I was good enough to beat them. Then I moved on to the next game, and the next, until my undefeated Bulldogs faced Tennessee. This was a high pressure matchup between two fake teams with fake championship aspirations. Tennessee beat me easily.

My hopes were destroyed, so I restarted the season. I beat Boise State again, then lost to South Carolina. Start over. Lose to Tennessee again. Start over. Beat Tennessee—lose to Florida. Start over. I repeated this cycle until my script finally played out, and I became a fake national champion.

The restart button is a great way to build fake football dynasties, but it only works in video games. There is no way to reset the world when life does not match our scripts. We are not entitled to our ambitions. Instead, we have to live in the tension between reality and those expectations. That tension is important. It is not, in itself, a bad thing. But we can also twist it into something dangerous. We are all prone to contort unmet expectations into jealousy, or to retreat from them altogether. Those spiritual movements can do real harm when the present disappoints.

That is one of the main reasons I wrote this book. So far my singleness has not matched the script I would have written. Unmet expectations have made disappointment an unwanted home. I know the pangs of frustration, impatience, and jealousy. Some elements of my singleness have been embarrassing. This is part of living a single life that God has given, but that I would not have chosen. Anyone who finds himself here will have to navigate this tension between the present and those unmet expectations.

The Bitter Gift of Disappointment

Obviously no one seeks disappointment. It brings no pleasure and serves no apparent purpose. Disappointment with God's gifts can easily grow into disappointment with him. Yet sometimes disappointment aptly describes our experience of submission to God and his will. It is not always a rebellion against what God has given. It can simply name the space between what God gives and what we desire.

Singleness is God's gift, and it is good. This desire for marriage is also good, and God-given. So this space between his gift and my expectations must be intended for good, too. If that is true, then this disappointment, like singleness and the desire that makes it difficult, is not a bog to escape. Nor does it necessarily flow from my failure or unbelief, though sometimes it does. (I have contributed to the perpetuation of this singleness more than anyone else)

Disappointment is not what threatens to destroy or embitter us. That dubious honor belongs to the jealousy that is so often parasitic to it. Disappointment can be eradicated, but only if those desires are eradicated too. But if those desires are God-given, then we do not have the right or the power to eliminate them. Instead, we have to allow disappointment to be our experience of unmet expectations. Enduring it can be a God-honoring response when the gifts and desires that God gives seem disjoined from each other. It does not mean that God has given poorly. Instead it means that he, not our ambitions, is the true object of our desires.

Desire's two traps (compromise and resignation) are clearly present here. Compromise seeks to alleviate disappointment by grasping for the immediate objects of desire, even if they are clearly not God-given. This could mean pursuing distorted desire (lust). Or it could mean a restless discontentment that refuses to receive what God offers. Instead of aiming through marriage toward union with Jesus, compromise lowers those expectations. It redirects those desires toward lesser things. It might exchange something great in the distance (eternal union with Jesus, made visible in marriage) for something smaller but closer. Or, it might settle for the distractions and entertainments that deaden our awareness of this tension in which we have to live. The danger may not be apparent, but it is real. Anything that might shield us from our unmet expectations will also bar us from real contentment. Compromise shrivels our capacity to receive what God gives. Even worse, it stunts our awareness of his nearness, and of our need for him.

Resignation goes a step further, abandoning those expectations altogether. It might try to stifle them, or to compartmentalize that disappointment for the sake of other goals. Busyness can become a repository for feelings or frustrations we would rather keep at bay. The hope for marriage itself could be treated as an obstacle to be cleared. These frustrated desires might hurt less if we could just keep them at a distance. This is especially tempting when an expectation seems less and less likely to be met.

Some of resignation's appeal lies in its apparent holiness. Laying aside a hope or desire for something God has not given sounds obedient. After all, faith requires that we receive what he gives. It refuses to grasp for the things he does not offer. However, resignation is not a movement of faith. It is a defense mechanism, not an offering to God. Avoiding the pain of disappointment by insulating myself from this desire for marriage is not an act of trust. It is a sad parody of control. It relinquishes good, hard longings in favor of a self-made promise of internal stability. That is escapism, masquerading as holiness.

There is no joy in resignation. Suppressing the hopes that flow from God-given desire offers no reward. It takes no faith to want nothing from life—or from God. If singleness is a gift that leads into deeper relation with God, then cauterizing those desires will also deaden our capacity for joy in the one who can actually meet them.[1]

God calls his people to contentment, something much more profound than resignation. Contentment recognizes the pain of unmet expectations. It even chooses to walk into that pain, rather than around it. It trusts that God's character is good and his promises are sure, even when he does not immediately meet those longings. Contentment gratefully receives all of God's gifts, even the unwanted ones. Most importantly, it remembers that these desires and expectations grow from a desperate need for communion with God. Even the desires that hurt are gifts meant to carry me into a deeper joy in him. Contentment receives those too, because it knows that God promises to meet his people in those waste places.

Kierkegaard called these the two movements of faith. By faith we open our hands to release the life we would otherwise hold onto. Then we keep those hands open to receive it again in even greater measure from God. It is better to stand before God with hands open, offering our desires and receiving whatever he gives in return, than to abandon those desires in resignation. What he gives is greater than anything we could take or make for ourselves. And in that releasing and receiving, we gain the assurance that our reward does not depend on our strength. Since God has given it, we are free from the burden of justifying our hold on it. We do not have to defend it. Instead, we can know that all that we have flows from the goodness of our unfailing God.[2] What

1. Kierkegaard, *Fear and Trembling*, 34–41.
2. Kierkegaard, *Fear and Trembling*, 39–41.

we have released and received again from him will never be lost, because Christ's victory is assured.

In my case, this has meant refusing to deny the difficulty of singleness. I cannot evade the loneliness and disappointment that have come with it. Nor should I. Those painful parts bear witness to something true. I was not made to be alone, and I need to remember that. Yet that memory is not a pigsty in which to wallow. It ought to push me toward the one who can fulfill those expectations. For all the control that resignation promises, only this move is fail-safe. The one who can truly satisfy has already given himself to me.

Disappointment is not the culprit for my failure to receive what God gives. Nor is it standing between me and joy. Bitterness and envy do. So do the shallow parodies of joy that I might substitute for my disappointment. These are the traps to avoid, not the discomfort of disappointment. Disappointment and joy must actually coexist. In fact, I find that disappointment is often the pathway into joy. It may not be an obvious path, and it certainly is not my preferred one. But disappointment is one of the tools God uses to draw us toward himself. God's presence often feels heaviest in the midst of unmet expectations. He has met me in the places where my need has been the clearest. In disappointment I have found that "in [his] presence there is fullness of joy" (Ps 16:11). I would not give up this disappointment for anything.

The Gift of Contentment

Living by faith requires loyalty to the life that God gives. That is hard, especially when the most beautiful moments actively fuel that disappointment. I live near several of my best friends from college, and we all attend the same church. We have grown together for years. Life has changed over time. Most of them are married with kids and advancing careers. Our gatherings include wives and babies and dogs and toys, none of them mine. I have watched them in each season of their lives. I saw them date, propose, marry, and move. I waited with them to become parents. At each milestone I celebrated with them. Sharing in their lives has been one of the greatest blessings of my own.

Those celebrations are also reminders that my life has taken another path. Every engagement, wedding, or birth can bring a pang of jealousy. We will celebrate together, and my waiting seasons my joy for them. But the celebrations also make that waiting heavier. Maybe this is not always envy, just uncertainty. To see it but not have it is hard. The main character in Marilynne Robinson's *Gilead* describes this well: "I believe the sin of covetise is that pang of resentment you may feel when even the people you love best have what you want and don't have."[3] I pray often for the capacity to celebrate these moments without jealousy. These times of celebration are some of the richest parts of my life, but that disappointment is always present.

Like marriage and singleness, contentment is impossible if it is not a gift too. We can seek and cultivate contentment, but we cannot conjure it for ourselves. I cannot will these longings into line. Contentment must begin outside us. This is a comfort. The God who gives gifts also gives us the ability to enjoy his gifts, even in the midst of struggle (Ecc 5:19). I have found that to be true.

Perhaps contentment is difficult because I actively reject it. I want something that will alleviate my disappointment, and contentment promises no such thing. In fact, it often comes in seasons of the most profound unrest. Prayer is the only proper arena for this struggle. I cannot walk into disappointment in my own strength. I do not have the power to redeem it. I can only carry it into God's throne room. What a gift when he chooses to answer our prayers with a "yes." But when he calls us to continue on the same path—disappointments and all—this too is a gift.

When we find ourselves in the middle of a storm, we typically seek shelter and hope the storm ends quickly. Contentment, however, will often look like sitting in a boat with Jesus while the storm still rages. As much as we want the storm to end, he would have us choose his presence over what looks like safety. Disappointment is a wind that blows us toward him, with all the waiting, uncertainty,

---

3. Robinson, *Gilead*, 134.

and wonder that comes with it. Even the pains of rejection and lone-liness flow into joyful rest in his presence and promise.

When we walk through pain knowing that God's promises are sure and his character is good, we walk by faith. We are never more like our savior than when we choose God and his gifts over the things we would grasp for ourselves. Jesus has already walked obediently into suffering. In that obedience he made a way for us to be called his brothers and sisters (Heb 2:11). Having suffered as one of us, he continues to sympathize with our weakness (Heb 4:15). He knows the pain of a lost friend (John 11). He knows the feeling of rejection and betrayal (Luke 22:61). He endured the pangs of loneliness and the dark night of abandonment (Luke 22:39–44). Our God has walked into suffering on our behalf. He chose to be one of us so that we would never suffer alone.

When we know that our God has walked into suffering, we see more clearly the true nature of his love. He is unfathomably beyond us, and yet Christ became one of us. By his Spirit he is in us and with us. His love takes the most transcendent and immanent forms. So we pray to a God who can do "far more abundantly than all that we ask or think" (Eph 3:20). We "with confidence draw near to the throne of grace" (Heb 4:16). We carry our burdens and our hurts to him because we know that Christ has already buried them. He knows the places in our hearts that feel barren. He sees the anxieties and shame that we would hide. He does not delight in that pain, but he does delight in the new life he will bring from it. He loves to hear the prayers that flow out of it. We have no need to cover our hurt or our longings because he knows them intimately. God raised Christ from the dead and sent us his Spirit so that we would never have to walk in them alone.

Disappointment can turn a feast to ash in your mouth. For all the parts of singleness I find beautiful I do not cherish the disap-pointment that comes with it. I also know that there is no content-ment in singleness without it. God has used this disappointment like a leash to draw me deeper into his love. It is making my heart into more fertile soil for contentment, and for a simple joy in the presence of my God. He has made the life I would not have scripted immeasurably rich, because he has given himself in it.

4

You Have Not Passed This Way Before

THERE ARE SEVERAL WAYS to summarize the story of the Bible. God the creator restores his broken creation. God the true bridegroom seeks and rescues his lost bride. God the just peacemaker reconciles his rebellious people to himself. Every one of these says more than we can comprehend, and less than the whole of God's work.

One theme that I have found particularly meaningful as a single person threads through all of those. The Bible tells of a humanity that has lost its home, and that desperately needs to return to it. The garden of Eden was our home once. God had given it to Adam and Eve as a place they could enjoy and cultivate. They lost that home when they disobeyed him. In their exile they carried the world's first homesickness. This new longing was not just a nostalgia for paradise, though they certainly felt that. It was more than a painful memory of what they had left behind. This homesickness contained seeds of hope that God had planted. He promised to restore all that they had lost. Still, this hopeful homesickness was not for the home they remembered. God would make a way for their return, but never to Eden as they knew it. Their homesickness had to carry them forward, not backward, because the future God promised would outshine their past.

The rest of the Bible tells this story. What began with home's loss will end with a homecoming: "Behold, the dwelling place of God is with man. He will dwell with them, and they will be his people, and God himself will be with them as their God" (Rev 21:3). We have inherited Adam and Eve's same homesickness for Eden, but that longing also anticipates a different home—eternity in his presence. This is the story's arc from Genesis to Revelation. It appears in Israel's journey to the promised land, in the filling of the tabernacle and temple with God's glory, and in Israel's return from the Babylonian exile. It shines with new light in the incarnation, when "the Word became flesh and dwelt among us" (John 1:14). It blazes like fire when the Spirit fills the disciples at Pentecost. Now it appears in the ordinary life of the church in union with Jesus. In Christ God is giving us a home in his presence, because in Christ God is making us his home.

Think of the comfort and peace that home has given you. That security only echoes the safety of God's presence. Think of the love and community you have known there. You have memories and experiences that you have shared and a life that you have lived together. You cannot separate your story from your mother's and father's, or from your brothers' and sisters'. Yet God has given himself to you more fully than anyone else you have ever loved. He has wrapped you into his story and bound you to his glory. Whatever you have known at home (or whatever you should have received but did not), God offers infinitely more in Christ.

And yet the promise of life in God's presence does not neutralize our desires for home here. We do not just long for the homes of our past or for an eternal one in front of us. We also want to create new homes, filled with that same kind of love. This third kind of homesickness is one of the more profound challenges in singleness. Home is something we want to build, and not by ourselves. Most of us expect home to be a place we share, and we want that sharing to be committed and continuous. It is a place we want to build so our people can be there.

John Ames, the main character in Marilynne Robinson's *Gilead*, lost his wife and child in labor. He spent several decades living alone until he remarried. He would amble through the familiar neighborhoods of his hometown, seeing lights in the windows and imagining a family life he had never known. Although this was a community he had known his whole life, he felt alienated from the people he passed. Even his best friend's family mystified him. His knowledge of Gilead and its people did not bridge the gap between his solitary bachelorhood and the family he missed. That alienation left him homeless in his hometown. He still remembered a family he had lost. He was home but homesick for a home he had only glimpsed.[1]

Sometimes I feel the same. I see other families and wonder what their homes are like. I often wish for it myself. I also wonder what home will mean for me if my singleness has no end. Most of my aspirations are not for achievements or possessions. They are for a home full of people to whom I have promised myself. That longing piques whenever I enter homes that are not mine, and every time I think about moving again. The home I am looking for may be new and unfamiliar, but the homesickness for it is real.

Anticipation

It may sound strange to speak of homesickness for a home you have never seen, but wandering Israel knew that feeling well. For Israel, home was a covenantal place that tied promise, community, and land together. God had promised their forefathers a land they would not claim for generations. They sojourned there, but it never fully belonged to them. Centuries later, Israel left Egypt for that same land. They carried those promises, and some ancestral memories, but this home of theirs was alien to them. When they finally reached it, they panicked. Their faith faltered and fear overwhelmed them. As a consequence, God led them to wander in the wilderness for forty years (Num 13–14).

---

1. Robinson, *Gilead*, 71.

When they finally returned to the banks of the Jordan River, God reminded them that in all their travels they had not passed that way before (Josh 3:4). This was a new time and place for them. For generations Israel had carried a homesickness for a home they had never known. Now they would enter the promised land they had envisioned for so long.

I love what God said to Israel, just before he fulfilled a promise their ancestors had awaited for generations: "You have not passed this way before" (Josh 3:4). It recognizes the unpredictability of obedience. Israel knew about this home, but they did not know how to enter it. The destination was promised, but the journey would unfold in unexpected ways. On the banks of the Jordan, Israel was almost home. Still, for all their wandering they had not passed that way before. They were not familiar with the land, or the people in it. They certainly did not know what the future would hold. They were strangers there, and that made crossing the threshold a daunting task. Even so, they knew that it would be home. The same God who led them through the wilderness would dwell with them there.

I would not call singleness a wilderness. There are wilderness places in my heart where singleness is a struggle, but singleness itself does not make this life an exile. Still, like Israel I have the hope of a home in front of me. There are promises, too, though there is no reason to think their fulfillment will meet my script. How could I know what to expect? I have no idea what is coming next, or how to handle it. Part of this is intrinsic to singleness, with its almost overwhelming range of possibilities. Everything is complicated and nothing is certain, but a family can at least pose answers for questions like "What must I prioritize?" or "Who will be here when I grow old?" I think a part of this homesickness stems from a longing for those obligations. Family can at least give shape to those expectations.

Any single person who hopes for marriage lives with that uncertainty. They have no idea if that desire will ever be met, or what it would look like if it were. I may walk the rest of my life carrying this gift of singleness. I do not know how the particular details of this story will pan out. I have not passed this way before. My anticipation comes from that place of wonder, in both senses of the word. I can wonder at the gift while also wondering what will happen next.

Of course, a family home is not the beginning of a life fully formed. Nor is it a destination that will satisfy those longings. The same was true of Israel's promised land. Both are signs pointing to our true home in the presence of God. Both homes, without that destination, prove underwhelming. Beneath our longings for earthly homes is an anticipation for that promised one. As we wait for both, he promises that he is enough. His presence had joined Israel as a flame and a cloud in their wandering. It settled with them in the tabernacle, and later in the temple. In each instance it foreshadowed an even greater divine dwelling to come. Now he gives us the down payment of the Holy Spirit and the fellowship of his church as foretastes of that fullness, too.

That presence does not make our longings for a literal home misplaced or misguided. Instead these earthly homes, like marriage and singleness, point toward that true end. This homesickness shapes our longings for our final home with him. God's promised presence, in turn, shapes the kind of home we look to build here. The task for the single person longing for a home, then, is not to establish one as quickly as possible. It is not to urgently populate a house, as though the only appropriate end for that desire must be immediate. Instead, it is to learn to live—and even to wait—in a way that aligns with that final home. That may mean building a nuclear family home here for the glory of God, should he give that. It may also mean waiting, even in the midst of uncertainty. It will certainly mean investing in whatever life God is giving, even as the window of opportunity for our own expectations diminishes.

Coming Home

At the end of *The Voyage of the Dawn Treader*, Aslan tells Edmund and Lucy that their adventures in Narnia are over. They have grown too old for Narnia, and must live in their own world now. That news sends Lucy into sobs. "It isn't Narnia, you know . . . It's *you*. We shan't meet *you* there. And how shall we live, never meeting you?" Aslan tells her that he will be with her there, too. She just has to know him by a different name.[2] For all our longings for another world, this world is home because Jesus meets us here.

You could say the same for singleness. It may not be the home that captivates our imaginations or dominates our dreams. It is not the Narnia of our favorite stories. Still, it points to promises and participates in a reality that exceeds what we can perceive. In Christ, God has made us into a new creation. Even more, he has made us his dwelling place. Home is in the presence of God, and singleness is one of the signs he has made to mark it.

Your singleness might end in this life. There may be a point in time when waiting yields to celebration. The God who has given so many gifts might give that new one. In the meantime, this singleness is a gift that must be received with gratitude. That means that the single life merits investment. It is not a short-term rental. It is an invitation to a permanent home. So, do the yard work and paint the walls. Set up a quiet place for reading and prayer. Build a big table for sharing. Plant trees that will bear fruit when you are old. Nothing poured into the single life will be wasted, even if singleness ends.

There is an important point built into that truth. Our final home will be in the new heavens and new earth, in God's presence. And, as we mentioned before, life in that home will be gloriously single. God has shaped the single life so that it can direct our longings toward that end. But he also calls us to wait for that future home by building the homes he gives now. That means more than the families or houses we may or may not have. Remember the union to which singleness points. God has formed us into a new family in Christ. You may feel a sense of homelessness as you long to build and share a home, but no Christian is truly homeless. You belong to the "household of God" (1 Tim 3:15). As Jesus said, "Whoever does the will of my Father in heaven is my brother and sister and mother" (Matt 12:50). Our home is in the presence

---

2. Lewis, *Voyage of the Dawn Treader*, 269–70.

of God together. In his church, he has given us a foretaste of the eternal, shared communion we anticipate.

Christian friendship and hospitality can make God's presence and love tangible now. I certainly have found that to be true. In the life of the church I have tasted that union. In my friends' homes I have seen glimpses of the new heavens and new earth. Those experiences have shaped my heart in ways that no intellectual understanding could. This "household of God" is the home in which he calls all of us to invest now. It is where our longings for union, intimacy, and companionship belong. He invites you to experience that here.

Jesus gives us a foretaste of our final home when he gathers us around his table. This bread and wine, just like our longings, remind us that he is present. We cannot desire his future, or his gifts, without also yearning to meet him in this world. The Eucharist itself reminds single people that Jesus has already fulfilled their hopes. The presence of Christ that we long for in the future is also enough for us now.

The point of all this is simple, even if the execution seems hard. This homesickness, just like all our desires, must lead us to desire him more deeply. That applies to our anticipation for that final home that he will make with us. It also applies to the access into his presence that he has given us in Jesus. Let your longings for a home stoke your eagerness for his coming. Let that eagerness for his coming break into the present with renewed desire for intimacy with him. Singleness has a home here, because he has made us his home.

5

Bigger on the Inside

WHAT IF AN AUTHOR could inhabit one of her stories? Would she? Should she? Would she see new layers in her characters? Would she stumble across patterns she never recognized and symbols she never intended? I think she would. But I also suspect the allure would wear off quickly. She would realize that the world she created had deep holes. It would be thin and shallow; living inside it would be cramped. The pieces would not quite fit. The same would be true for all of her characters. Even a writer like Tolkien—the architect of as expansive a world as one could imagine—would find that there is a wonder to creaturely life that cannot be replicated. A finite imagination cannot tread there.

We all try, though. The temptation to script our own lives seduces all of us. Who would not want to edit the parts of our lives that we would rather skip? Who would not want to sketch out the path to their dreams or ambitions and see them through to the end? That is a normal desire. But if I could fashion my own life for myself, would it be worth living? Would it meet my idealized expectations, or would my narrow imagination and inattention to detail leave me with a caricature of the life I would want? Do I have enough creativity, intelligence, or wisdom to give myself what I need? Could I possibly create a life big enough to inhabit? We misremember our pasts, misunderstand our presents, and misjudge our futures, but we would still make ourselves the authors of our own stories. Disappointment only strengthens that impulse.

Faith, on the other hand, entails a willingness to live the lives God has given. It requires a submission that flows from a child-like dependence on God. It yields a willingness to accept the places God gives us in his world, whatever they may be. For all my efforts to mold the world and my story to my wishes, life itself is more profound than anything I could conceive. We have to release our obsession with control—the need to script our own stories—and instead learn to live the lives that God gives.

I think about that with regards to singleness. There are things that I hope for and even try to plan for. I want to be married and have kids. I have some firm ideas about the character of the woman I would marry, and some softer ideas about what she might look like and enjoy. I have even attached those ideas and hopes to specific people. Of course, those hopes do not always maintain their original shape. There is certainly no assurance that those hopes will be reciprocated. In the midst of uncertainty, only two things have been clear: my singleness is not wholly subject to my plans, and I do not get to craft my own exit strategy. If my life (including this singleness) is like a story, then I am not the author.

Singleness, Control, and a Greater Story

This story metaphor is tricky, because none of our stories are self-contained. They all conflict with each other. Each one weaves in and out of all the rest. That tangled web is one of the reasons we cannot control our narratives. It is also one reason that postmodern thought has rejected the idea of a single, uniting story. It recognizes that the uniqueness of individual experiences makes comprehensive knowledge impossible. It also says that there is no uniting story to know anyway. Every attempt to create one has resulted in the exaltation of a few and the oppression of all the rest. Postmodernism has helpfully realized that modernity's story of human progress has failed to keep most of its promises. Modernity offered a vision of prosperity built on human potential, science, and trade. But its overarching narrative flattened the world into a field of resources ripe for harvest. In other words, it turned cosmic mysteries into an industrial grocery list. At its worst it devoured humans for the sake of progress, leading to a spectrum of atrocities ranging from genocide and nuclear holocausts to subtler indecencies like corporate oligarchy and syndicated talk radio. Broadly speaking, postmodernism has responded to the inadequacy of modernity's story by rejecting all overarching narratives. This is probably both postmodernism's greatest strength and most damning flaw. It did the world a fine service by undermining the ideological frameworks that made human reason absolute and technological progress an unassailable good. However, it also over-learned its lesson. Modernity's sin was not its adherence to a greater story, but its commitment to the wrong one.

Yet Christianity insists that there is a story that enfolds all the stories of the world (including singleness) into itself. God is reconciling the world to himself in Jesus Christ (2 Cor 5:19). This is the story that gives everything its meaning, and it will not bend to our wills or desires. God is generous with us, but not on our terms. Our lives will only make sense if we first receive this story that comes from outside ourselves. We cannot understand singleness without seeing how it fits within the story of Jesus' victory over sin and death.

The main character in this story is a God who is not threatened by evil or quarantined by his own holiness. Rather, he is intensely personal. He is one God in three eternally united persons, and he is three persons eternally united as one God. And, to our great benefit, God the Father, Son, and Holy Spirit has been working to bring salvation to the world since Adam and Eve brought sin and death into it. To do that, this already mysterious triune God willed another equally astounding mystery. The same God who made all things and "in [whom] all things hold together" (Col 1:17), stepped inside his creation as a creature. He took human flesh and dwelt among us (John 1:14), living a human life and dying a human death. He walked in our weakness (Heb 4:15), suffered pain, endured loss, wept (John 11:35), and faced abandonment (Mark 15:34). We can call his story the beginning of ours because God has folded the story of humanity into his own.

The one who stood as Adam's substitute in the garden (Matt 26:36–46) and as Israel's substitute in the wilderness (Matt 4:1–11) stands as our substitute now. He lived a life of perfect obedience. He succeeded as God's true image-bearer where Adam, Israel, and all of humanity failed. On the cross he died as the atoning substitute for the world. He bore the punishment for sin in his body, so that in his body death itself could be undone. The resurrected and ascended Christ continues to live as our substitute. He stands before the Father on our behalf (Heb 7:25) and replaces our death with his resurrection (Gal 2:20). The narrative of the Old Testament continues: God's Son died, but God raised him to life.[1] And this new life is not reserved for him alone. The Spirit unites to Christ all who believe this story and receive this gift (Eph 4:3–6). Those who were once God's enemies can stand before the Father as his children (John 1:12; Heb 4:14–16). Jesus' substitution gives us his place in the story. He has joined us to himself, so that he can bring us into the life and love of God. Singleness points to that glorious reality—union with God in Jesus, by the power of the Holy Spirit. That trumps anything the world or our own imaginations could offer.

This is the story that makes contentment in the midst of waiting and disappointment possible. That broader story of God renewing and restoring all things is our grounds for believing that he will do the same with us. Only the gospel can give us the assurance we need to receive our smaller stories, too.

I use "receive" intentionally there. Learning to be single may mean inhabiting a story we would not want to read, even less live. I have never wanted to be single. I have dreamed dreams, laid plans, assigned hopes, and tried to stammer my way out of it many times. Some of those plans, though certainly not all, were good and wise. They sought to honor God and others. They were not hopes to be

---

1. Jenson, *Theology in Outline*, 11–12.

ashamed of or to hide. Some of them were good plans that I ruined. Others failed immediately—and for good reason. I have never succeeded in writing the story I wanted for myself. None of those plans ever came to pass, and as one after another was denied a danger grew. It was not the threat of wasted time or missed opportunity. It was the danger of a heart hardening against what God was giving. Many of you have likely found yourselves in the same place. If so, then you have come face-to-face with a truth that seems hard to bear, but that is actually loaded with good news.

There is only one creator. God alone has the power to fashion from nothing. Only he can change without restriction what he has made, or say without contingency what the future will hold. He allows humans to be sub-creators. We can make and work and fashion and plan within the parameters he grants to us. But we cannot make from nothing, and we can only follow our own plans as far as he allows. That means that we cannot be the creators of our own good or the authors of our own lives. We cannot configure anything for ourselves that would exceed what he has given. Whether we will it or not, we are subject to the will of the one who made us. This is true with regards to my singleness and to everything else.

That is another idea with little purchase in our culture, but it is unavoidable here. Nothing truly good comes from grasping for what he does not offer, or from turning away what he has provided. Whatever we might build for ourselves will not match what he extends to us. This does not mean that whatever is given in the present must be received permanently. In the case of singleness, it does not take marriage off the table. It does not prohibit some initiative while we wait for God to give it. It simply means that only God has the power to form a life worth living. He is the author of the best stories. We will only find our greatest good within the story he gives, even if a singleness you do not want is part of the script. There will be no joy or satisfaction in striving for what God has not given or in wiggling out of this gift he is giving now. This important truth is not limited to the single life, but it is especially visible from here. The stories God gives are the only ones worth living.

We could never have imagined a God who shows his greatness by taking a tiny human form or who bridges the immeasurable abyss between his being and ours by becoming one of us. This is a story we could not have written, and yet here we are. We live given lives in a given world, broken but wonderful because he has made it and entered it. As paradoxical as it may seem, this is the only kind of story that can give life and the world their meaning. It is the story that gives singleness its meaning, too.

Expectations in the Ruins

As glorious as that story is, living inside it is still a struggle. Jesus has not yet expelled the evil, ugliness, and suffering that fill our world. We experience glimpses and foretastes of his resurrection life now, but we still wait for Christ to fully usher in his new creation. Until then, the world will continue to be a place of disappointment and heartache. In that disappointment we will see the painful underside of a world of wonder outside our control. The world is indeed too great to fit inside the scripts we would give it. We must in turn live lives and experience pains we would never want.

No one can choose if they will pass through adversity, or how it might play out. If I wrote my own script, I would keep some of it. After all, the conflict is what frames us as heroes in our own stories. I would curate those struggles to cast myself in the best light. I might even model my story's development after Joseph's. After being sold into slavery by his brothers and later falsely imprisoned, Joseph saved Egypt and his family from famine. He died the most second powerful man in Egypt. It would be so gratifying to say to the world what Joseph told his brothers: "As for you, you meant evil against me, but God meant it for good" (Gen 50:20). It is easier to accept the things we do not want when we can see their resolution, or at least glimpse their integration into a larger story. Singleness would be easier to walk through if I could see its happy ending.

Sometimes I fear my story will look more like Jeremiah's. He was called to preach a message of judgment mixed with hope to

Judah, but Judah's leaders opposed him at every turn. His obedience to God resulted in slander, house arrest, and confinement in a mud pit. After Babylon destroyed Jerusalem, those left behind kidnapped Jeremiah and carried him to Egypt, where he likely died. Though Jeremiah remained faithful, his death never saved Judah. The hope he proclaimed was always far in the future. God would restore his exiled people to their land, but only after seventy years of exile. Jeremiah did not live to see that day. God never tied a neat little bow from the loose ends of Jeremiah's life. He just died without seeing the future God promised through him.

In the midst of all that discouragement, God never promised Jeremiah a happy ending. Instead he promised his continued presence and the companionship of one or two friends. But the full story shows that this was enough. God did faithfully sustain Jeremiah, all the way to the end. His presence and promises gave Jeremiah the grounds to invest in the ruins of his fractured home.[2] God does the same for us now. The Bible does not spell out exactly how God will use our hardships for his purposes (though it is clear that he will). We do not see God tying all the world's loose ends together. In fact, we do not see much at all. If what we see is all we have, then evil is impregnable and pain is irredeemable. We may wonder why he allows it to persist. Still, we know that God's answer for evil is to undo it from within. Jesus has walked miles in our shoes. He knows our weakness because he suffered it. Now Jesus calls us his brothers and sisters—not because we have overcome our weakness, but because he has entered into it (Heb 2:10).

When we see our stories within this greater story, we can glimpse how even the disappointment of unwanted singleness invites us to see our redeemer walking with us. My singleness has hardly been tragic or unfair. No one has grievously sinned against me or wounded me. Still, in singleness I have seen how easily disappointment and envy can fill the distance between my hopes and the reality that God has given. I have been challenged most directly in that place of tension and unmet expectation. Like Jeremiah, I have also found that God delights in showing his

2. House, "Investing in the Ruins," 12–13.

faithfulness in disappointment. He is teaching me to be content when the gifts he gives are the gifts I would leave behind. Without this disappointment I could not have learned that the singleness I would reject is aimed at my good.

This is part of what it means to live as a fallen person in a fallen world. Still, God is not flippant about these sources of pain in our hearts. He means for these wilderness places to be places of renewal for us, just as they were for Israel (Isa 35). They are the sites where the transforming power of his Word and Spirit will bring life out of death. We may loathe or fear these dark, arid waste spaces. We would certainly avoid them if we could. But they are precisely where God promises to meet us and to sustain us.

The gospel does not erase the ache of anticipation or the sting of rejection. Instead it promises that God is good in the midst of that. The story he tells is better. It gives hope for an indescribable future and comfort in a lonely present. It even declares that my own story is a gift. All of its discouragement, rejection, gaffes, waiting, and wondering cannot overshadow the beauty of all God has offered. The gospel is a story of God winning the life of the world from a tragedy darker than anything I have ever known. The cross and resurrection show God making new life from death. My singleness has new meaning in this story of a God who turns emptiness into fullness. If God has already taken the worst this world can offer and transformed it into new life, then I can expect him to turn my deepest disappointments into soil for even greater joys. The gardener in this story loves to transform seasons of pain and loneliness into something beautiful.

It is hard to wait, and to struggle with the sense of lost time as it passes. I feel it when I watch my friends' children grow, and when I watch my own family grow older. I want a taste of what my friends have, and for my parents to know the joy of grandchildren. Contentment in the present moment is a hard enough thing. Contentment as time marches on is yet another. The impatience and restlessness that grow so easily often nudge me toward envy rather than gratitude. But there is a theme that surfaces repeatedly throughout scripture that is particularly meaningful here. God offers himself, and the world that he is redeeming, to those who wait for him. Think of the time that passed between the prophecies that pointed to Christ and his actual coming. Consider all the people who died still hoping for the restoration of Israel and the advent of their Messiah. We have not felt our hearts skip like Simeon's when he saw Jesus in the temple—"Lord, now you are letting your servant depart in peace, according to your word; for my eyes have seen your salvation" (Luke 2:29–30). God did not fail any of those people who waited—even if, unlike Simeon, they never got to see the Messiah they hoped for face-to-face. The story of God's redemption often moves slowly, but there is an important assurance communicated to us in that truth. Patience is not wasted time in God's kingdom.

Even with that hope, this is still a challenging place to stand. God's promises do not free my singleness from unmet longings. Nor do they make disappointment sting any less. In fact, those same promises warn us not to expect discipleship to follow any other path. We follow Jesus, who "for the joy that was set before him" (Heb 12:2) set his face like flint toward the cross (Luke 9:51). Likewise, Jesus told his disciples to take up their crosses and follow him (Luke 9:23). Walking in faithful singleness can sometimes be a challenging cross to bear. There is loneliness, uncertainty, and temptation involved. But the difficulty of singleness does not mean that God is withholding something good. Nor is the frustration of God-given desires evidence that God has defaulted on his promises. Jesus has borne the consequences I should reap for the times I fail to walk in singleness faithfully. He will banish the disappointment and hurt that fill parts of it. While we look forward to the story's end, he calls us to live out the stories he gives us now. We can do so, knowing that we do not walk in them alone.

This is one of the many places where singleness can be a microcosm of the Christian life. It is not that singleness is unique; it simply provides a particular vantage point. It is a place we might rather avoid but that nevertheless offers a distinct view of God's goodness and an invitation into his presence. Unmet expectations can be the soil from which joyful contentment grows when the otherwise unattainable end is already promised. We do not go anywhere Christ has not gone first or without the Spirit whom he has sent. That fact alone enables us to walk in this world of uncertainty with wonder rather than despair. It allows us to receive those God-given parts of our lives that cause us to ache, like singleness, with gratitude.

Let your desire for marriage lead you to embrace God's gift of himself and give yourself in communion with brothers and sisters in Christ. The single life shaped by God's promises does not cauterize its longings. It does not abandon God's gifts for romantic baubles and trifles that only vaguely echo what your heart desires. Rightly oriented desire will not draw you away from singleness at all, at least not until God gives something different. It will draw you deeper into the single life as you run toward the God who gives himself in it.

As for the present, this world is still wonderful precisely because it is given. More than that, it is wonderful because the God who gave it has given himself in it. He promises to sustain us as we walk and as we wait. By entering into this story he has made it bigger on the inside—large and thick and real enough to be truly inhabitable. Even with its brokenness, we could never create a world greater than the one God spoke into being and filled with his presence. We could certainly never write a story more abundant or generous than his overarching story of resurrection. The same is true for my story. This single life is the story I must be loyal to, because the God who gives it also gives himself. He has proven time and time again that he is enough.

Conclusion: Roads, Paths, and the Single Life

IN HIS ESSAY "A Native Hill," Wendell Berry makes an insightful distinction between roads and paths. Roads are for movement, not enjoyment. They bypass obstacles and speed through leveled landscapes at breakneck speeds. They flatten time and space to carry people from one location to another. But they never serve as places in themselves. No one slowly savors I-95. Emptiness is the road's virtue.[1]

We often talk of singleness like an empty space that only exists to be crossed. This frames singleness as a waypoint or a threshold to be crossed. That sort of singleness could be treated with the same flippancy as a short-term lease. No one invests in a property they rent. You might not decorate a house you are ready to leave.

If a road speeds through singleness, a path walks into it and through it. A path is not just a means to an end. Rather than flattening the landscape, it participates in it. The path itself is an experience. It enters a world of irregularity that will not be ignored or hurried. It may not climb over an obstacle in front of it. Instead, it allows the obstacle to shape the journey. Paths let nature's inconveniences belong where they are. Without them the landscape is scarred and barren, robbed of its beauty. A hiker on a path can

1. Berry, "Native Hill," 12.

savor the pleasure of the journey itself. She treats its dangers with appropriate respect. She checks the weather, packs extra water, and carries bear spray. But she will not exchange the sound of birds or the smell of wet leaves for security or efficiency.[2]

This kind of singleness is not a highway that ushers us into whatever tidy futures we would chart for ourselves. It accepts these twists, turns, climbs, and descents, even the obstacles and disappointments, as crucial parts of the gift.

This does not mean that the path ignores its destination. The path's end does not erase the joy of the journey. In fact, it supplies it. Anticipation for the end gives the path a meaning it could never have on its own. The weariness of the journey strengthens that longing for its destination. That promised joy offers a present joy, even when the journey is a slog. Hope shapes how we enjoy God's good gifts, even in a broken, sorrowful present. It teaches me how to receive singleness as the gift that it is, even when I long for a marriage feast of my own.

The "path" image is a helpful one for envisioning Christian singleness. I might marry one day. I wonder what that would look like. At a single point in time waiting might become receiving and anticipation might yield to celebration. The God who has given so many gifts might give that new one. If I could speed through singleness as fast as I could to get to that point, I probably would.

But the path does not allow for that. It will not permit that sort of destructive, oblivious rush. A traveler on a path cannot exchange the life God has given for a more expedient journey. He can only walk the path that is there.

In this case, the path and the road are not different ways to arrive at the same place. They have different destinations. If marriage is the end, then singleness can only be a road. It is just a waypoint. There is no sense in investing in it, or in treating the road itself with care. It points to nothing. Its only value is speed and emptiness, because the destination has nothing to offer the journey. It can only give the hope of its end. God forbid that that end should disappoint.

2. Berry, "Native Hill," 12.

Singleness has a destination that is greater and richer than marriage. Union with God in Jesus Christ by the Holy Spirit. That might lie at the end of a slower path, but it gives meaning to the entire journey. It even breaks into the journey in mysterious ways. God is not waiting to meet you at your destination. If you take the highway you will speed past him. Instead he promises to meet you where the path is darkest, rainiest, and scariest.

None of this should quench your desire for marriage if you have it. It should deter you from seeing singleness as a checkpoint on the way to maturity. The single life is not a challenge to be conquered en route to a fuller life. Singleness is not a prerequisite to marriage on some imagined progression. Singleness and marriage are two parallel streams. They both flow in the same direction—union with Jesus. When we say singleness is a gift, this is what we must mean. The single life is a means by which God draws us into deeper intimacy with himself.

So, with all that said, learn to love your singleness, even if you are trying to end it. Let your desires for marriage spur you to delight in Jesus. He is the only one who can satisfy your longings. Rest in the promises of God's presence by building a home in this singleness. Treat it as a path that merits a respect and delight of its own. Cherish even the unmet desires and disappointments. What he offers is better than anything you could imagine.

Bibliography

Augustine. *Confessions*. Translated by Henry Chadwick. Oxford: Oxford University Press, 2008.

Berry, Wendell. "A Native Hill." In *The Art of the Commonplace: The Agrarian Essays of Wendell Berry*, 3–31. Berkeley, CA: Counterpoint, 2002.

Chesterton, G. K. *Orthodoxy*. Garden City, NY: Image, 1959.

House, Paul. "Investing in the Ruins: Jeremiah and Theological Vocation." *Journal of the Evangelical Theological Society* 56.1 (2013) 5–15.

Jenson, Robert W. *A Theology in Outline: Can These Bones Live?* New York: Oxford University Press, 2016.

Kierkegaard, Soren. *Fear and Trembling*. Edited by C. Stephen Evans and Sylvia Walsh. Translated by Sylvia Walsh. Cambridge: Cambridge University Press, 2006.

Lewis, C. S. *The Voyage of the Dawn Treader*. New York: Harper Trophy, 1980.

———. "The Weight of Glory." In *The Weight of Glory and Other Addresses*, 25–46. London: William Collins, 2013.

Mascall, E. L. *Christ, the Christian, and the Church: A Study of the Incarnation and Its Consequences*. Peabody, MA: Hendrickson, 2017.

Robinson, Marilynne. *Gilead*. New York; Picador, 2004.

———. "Imagination and Community." In *When I Was a Child I Read Books*, 19–33. New York: Picador, 2012.

Schmemann, Alexander. *For the Life of the World*. Yonkers, NY: St. Vladimir's Seminary Press, 2018.